COLUMNS BY THE SEA

THE ROPER HOUSE

The Roper House, circa 1838 on the High Battery, Charleston, S.C., painted by Felix Kelly.

COLUMNS BY THE SEA

THE ROPER HOUSE

CHARLESTON, S.C.

By

RICHARD HAMPTON JENRETTE

Classical American Homes
Preservation Trust

Published by
Classical American Homes Preservation Trust
69 East 93rd Street
New York, NY 10128

www.classicalamericanhomes.org

Contents © 2013 Classical American Homes Preservation Trust

Design: Donald Giordano

Printed and bound in the United States of America.

Library of Congress Control Number: 2013953352

ISBN 978-0-9825737-1-6 paperback

A vintage photograph of Roper House, probably taken in the early 1880's, after its post-Civil War restoration by the Siegling family, who owned the house for 56 years.

HOW I ACQUIRED ROPER HOUSE

It was a balmy moonlight evening — back in 1968 — when I first saw the Roper House in Charleston, South Carolina. It was love at first sight — a love affair with an old house that continues to this day, more than 45 years later. The massive two-story Ionic columns, glittering in the moonlight, were the biggest I had ever seen on a private residence. They seemed even taller standing on top of a high-arched pedestal base, flanking the first floor. The location of the house on the Battery afforded an unobstructed view out to the Atlantic Ocean.

I came across Roper House while visiting Charles and Carol Duell, clients of our New York investment firm (Donaldson, Lufkin & Jenrette). The Duells lived only a few doors away in another magnificent early 19th Century town house. When I told them how smitten (and that was the right word) I was by the Roper House, Charlie told me "It just might be for sale." While I was not at all looking to buy a house, I could not resist an invitation the next day to meet the owner, Drayton Hastie, whose elderly mother occupied the principal floor of the house (the other two floors were rented). The price seemed reasonable, probably because the house would come with a life tenancy for Drayton's mother, then aged 76. Although I was fully occupied in New York at the time, I decided to buy Roper House as an investment, thinking it would one day make a great retirement home in my old age. Mrs. Hastie's life tenancy was actually a plus for me since I had no need for a home in Charleston at that point of my life.

Early morning sunrise light the Roper House. Below, Dick Jenrette and Roper House columns.

As some of you who read this already know, my love affair with Roper House was just the beginning of what has turned out to be a fascinating lifetime career of restoring classical American homes of this period — the first half of the 19th Century. The Charleston experience also enhanced my appreciation of the value and importance of historic preservation. I've tried to share this experience with others, and the six historic properties that I have restored are all scheduled to be given to Classical American Homes Preservation Trust, which was set up to take ownership and open them to the public. In this endeavor, my role model was the late Frances Edmunds in Charleston and her beloved Historic Charleston Foundation. Frances didn't do it all single handedly, but in my eyes she saved Charleston's now famous historic district, which has inspired so many communities all over the nation.

So I am a confirmed "house-aholic" and would like to share some of these tales of historic preservation with you. Please consider this book just an introduction to the Roper House, written casually by me. One of these days I hope someone else will do a more scholarly research job, which would reveal more about what life was like for the families that have lived in this wonderful old house over two centuries. Meanwhile, the grandeur of Roper House speaks for itself.

Dick

Richard H. Jenrette
November 7, 2013

Columns by the Sea—

Background on the Roper House

The first house I owned outright (excluding a New York City co-op) was the Roper House, a magnificent Greek Revival mansion at 9 East Battery in Charleston, South Carolina. I bought it in 1968, the 130th anniversary of the house's completion in 1838 and just short of my own fortieth birthday. Although I did not realize it at the time, this purchase was the beginning of my hobby of collecting old houses and antiques, which continues unabated forty-five years later. The fact that I did not begin my acquisitive habits until age forty is evidence that you don't have to be a *wunderkind* to start your own collection.

The Roper House, with its magnificent Ionic columns overlooking the sea, seemed to me the quintessential antebellum mansion that my *Gone With the Wind*-influenced generation dreamed about owning, although Roper House is a town house and not a plantation. Not only is the house stunning architecturally, it has an unsurpassed location at the head of Charleston's High Battery, a gigantic sea wall built in the early nineteenth century to reclaim swampy land and hold back floods and hurricanes. From the great piazza of the Roper House, one looks out directly over Charleston Harbor to Fort Sumter, where the Civil War began, and beyond that to the Atlantic Ocean. There is even a piece of the barrel of the largest Confederate cannon, which blew up in front of the house, embedded in the roof, where it has remained since 1865. And, of course, Charleston itself is one of the prettiest cities in America. For in-city living, you could not find a better location or a more elegant house architecturally — at least that is my boast. I've never found a town house anywhere — including London, Paris or New York — that matches the Roper House from an all-around point of view.

It is a tradition in Charleston to call houses by their builder's name. Robert William Roper, the builder, was a planter whose father, Thomas Roper, had built and owned an earlier, less imposing town house still standing a block or so further up East Battery. The Ropers claimed direct descent from Margaret Roper, a daughter of Sir Thomas More. Robert William Roper, who married Martha Rutledge Laurens, was a

The double front doors of Roper House, facing the Atlantic Ocean, open inside to a welcoming red carpet and a classical circular staircase.

civic leader, elected to the State legislature and chairman of the important Agriculture Committee (cotton being the most important crop). He was also quite articulate, judging by several of his speeches which were published in pamphlet form. In one celebratory Fourth of July speech (when that occasion was more popular in the South before the Civil War), Roper boasts about America's growing roster of prominent native artists. His list of American artists, including John Trumbull, Gilbert Stuart, Charles Willson Peale and Thomas Sully, was remarkably prescient, judging by the number that have stood the test of time and remain popular today. Roper's wife, Martha Rutledge Laurens, also had a distinguished South Carolina lineage. Her grandfather, John Rutledge, was the state's first Governor during the American Revolution. His brother, Edward Rutledge, was a signer of the Declaration of Independence and also a Governor.

The Roper wealth seemed to come from their plantation — Point Comfort — about fifteen miles up the Cooper River, which empties into Charleston Harbor right in front of the Roper House (a site that Charlestonians, only halfway in jest, describe as "where the Cooper River and the Ashley River come together to form the Atlantic Ocean"!).

The architect of Roper House has not been positively identified. Architectural historians Kenneth and Martha Severens, in their definitive article on Roper House for *The Magazine ANTIQUES*, make a persuasive case for Charles Friedrich Reichardt, a Prussian architect and pupil in Berlin of Germany's greatest classical architect Karl Friedrich Schinkel. Reichardt arrived in Charleston in 1836, and was the architect of the monumental Charleston Hotel. Roper House was built about the same time. Both the Charleston Hotel and Roper House bear strong resemblance to Schinkel's much-praised Altes Museum (1822-30) in Berlin, with its long Ionic colonnade and flat roofline, built high above a ground-level arcade. Roper may also have used a local architect, possibly Frederic Wesner, to complete the work, but I believe that Reichardt influenced the bold design of the house. Reichardt's work at the Charleston Hotel also was the genesis of Nathaniel Potter's plans for Millford Plantation (1840-42), which I acquired later in 1992. In terms of architectural detail, Millford is even grander than Roper House, but lacks the spectacular view overlooking Charleston's harbor.

Like most Charleston houses, Roper House is built with its gable end, or side, directly on the street, with a long piazza to catch sea breezes built along the length of

Upper left to clockwise: Robert William Roper, his wife Martha Rutledge Roper, and her grandfather John Rutledge, South Carolina's first governor during the American Revolution.

A portrait of George Washington, by Harriet Cany Peale, a Washington memorial clock made by Dubuc á Paris, and a statue of Lafayette by Houdon are featured in the high-ceilinged front parlor.

15

the house, sideways to East Battery. But the similarity to other Charleston houses largely stops there. Charleston's heyday as one of America's four largest and richest cities was in the late eighteenth century, and many of the great houses in this neighborhood were built prior to or just after 1800 in a more restrained "Adam style", a Charleston version of Britain's Adam brothers' Georgian style. In contrast, Roper House was built in the much more exuberant Greek Revival style some forty years later when Charleston was seeking to make an economic comeback after steadily losing ground to its northern port rivals — New York, Boston, Philadelphia, and Baltimore. The two-story Ionic columns of the Roper House, built on top of an arched loggia across the side of the ground floor, are much larger than the delicate columns found on most earlier Charleston residences. The effect is far more robust, almost boastful.

Indeed, Robert William Roper had wanted his house to be the first and most prominent to be seen as visitors approached Charleston by sea (ships still were the most important means of travel in the early nineteenth century). At the time the High Battery was completed, the Roper mansion was the first house to be built, standing alone in a large corner plot that is now shared with three other large antebellum mansions — the DeSaussure House, now on the corner, and two Ravenel houses on either side of Roper House. The worldwide financial panic of 1837 (cotton prices collapsed) might have induced Roper to sell some of his choice land. Another local explanation is that Roper's father gave away much of the family fortune to found Roper Hospital (a vibrant Charleston institution today), forcing the son to economize on his dream house. Yet the scale and magnificence of the giant Ionic columns that Roper built give the house precedence over its neighbors. Roper House still evokes a gasp of surprise at its massive scale from visitors who pass by today.

Porthole Portrait of George Washington, painted circa 1850, by Harriet Cany Peale, copied from her father-in-law, Charles Wilson Peale's original portrait of Washington.

A House With a Charleston Grande Dame

When I bought Roper House from Drayton Hastie in 1968 I agreed to a life tenancy for his mother, Sarah Hastie, then in her late seventies and said to be in poor health. Under the agreement Mrs. Hastie would have use of the *piano nobile* — the principal, or second floor of the mansion (with eighteen-foot-high ceilings!) — for the rest of her life. At this time there were two rental units on the ground floor (in what had been the dining room, library and kitchen) and a full floor-through apartment on the third, or bedroom floor, which I could use for myself as a *pied-à-terre* in Charleston.

Since I didn't need such a large house in Charleston, and was fully occupied with my work in New York, this arrangement worked exceedingly well, although Mrs. Hastie lived to be ninety — a long time for a life tenancy. When I came to Charleston on weekends, the handsome top floor apartment that Anthony Hail decorated for me was certainly adequate for my needs. The deck we built on the roof still has the best view in Charleston out to the Atlantic Ocean.

I also became very fond of Mrs. Hastie, whose elegant lifestyle epitomized the best of Charleston living. Tall and commanding in presence, she dressed in a long velvet evening gown *every* evening before dinner, whether or not she had guests. Miriam, her maid, would offer up the ritual evening bourbon, and Mrs. Hastie would hold court. As a native Charlestonian living right in the city in such handsome quarters, she never lacked for visitors. I recall her advising me to give my parties there at full moon, which rises in a giant orange ball out of the sea right in front of Roper House, shimmering on the water. Of all my houses and other places visited, I can recall no better place to experience the rising of the full moon.

Mrs. Hastie seemed to enjoy her final years to age ninety at Roper House. She kept right on top of current events, had a parade of amusing callers, and the staff to handle them. I recall thinking that this was the perfect retirement home — mild climate, an attractive city, attractive neighbors and interesting out-of-town visitors to Charleston, the availability of help, and excellent medical facilities at the Medical University of South Carolina as well as the house's namesake Roper Hospital.

Another view of the front parlor, or piano nobile, *located on the second floor, overlooking Charleston Harbor.*

Next spread, a view of the piano nobile *from the rear parlor, with views of the Atlantic Ocean from tall floor-to-ceiling windows. Formerly gas-lit chandeliers were made especially for Roper House after the Civil War.*

Mrs. Hastie's Replacement – My Own Mother

After Mrs. Hastie passed away, I spent about two years updating and modernizing Roper House, anticipating that I would make greater personal use of it. But it was not to be — yet. My own mother (Emma Love Jenrette), having turned age ninety about the time work was complete on the house, was no longer able to live alone in her home in Florida. Unable to get help for her there and unwilling to put her in a nursing home, my sister, brother and I concluded that the best solution would be to move Mother into Roper House, taking over part of the top floor that I had kept as an apartment. An added inducement was the presence in Charleston of my nephew, Dr. Joseph M. Jenrette III, at the Medical University of South Carolina. This insured excellent medical attention for her, although she rarely needed it.

The arrangement seemed to work well, and Mother lived to be 101 before she passed away quietly one night. At her advanced age, and not being a Charleston native, she was never able to enjoy the Roper House as Mrs. Hastie had done before her. But the presence of four loyal nurse's aides, operating on three shifts, made life comfortable for her.

Because of my full-time business involvement in New York and the other "second homes" I later bought, I was never bothered by not having full access to Roper House either during Mrs. Hastie's long life tenancy or Mother's subsequent passing the century mark in age there. But I did begin to think I also would have to live to be ninety to get to enjoy the place fully. I am now eighty-four and still not living there full-time, so on to age ninety!

The tall French case clock, circa 1810, is similar to a Napoleon clock at Malmaison outside Paris. The clock was purchased in 1981 by Mr. Jenrette from another old Charleston home, where it had remained since the late 19th century. Located in the second floor hallway, the clock fills the narrow space between the two doors into the double parlors.

An early portrait of Andrew Jackson, by Ralph E.W. Earl, was painted in 1823 after Jackson's victory in the Battle of New Orleans and before he became President. The portrait is unusual with a gold frame and crimson swags painted on the canvas.

Decorating the Roper House

While Mother lived on the top floor, I did proceed with plans to renovate the first two floors, including Mrs. Hastie's beloved *piano nobile* with its double parlors and eighteen-foot-high ceilings. David Byers and Browne & Company, of Atlanta, who had recently done curtains at both The White House and State Department, created stunning deep blue and gold draperies for the giant floor-to-ceiling windows, which looked out to sea. Bill Thompson designed, and Scalamandré produced, new wall-to-wall carpets (which came into vogue about the time Roper House was built) also in blue and gold, with classical motifs matching the architecture. The walls throughout the house were *faux*-marbleized by Robert Jackson, a decorating technique that was popular in the early 19th century.

The double parlors of the *piano nobile*, each outfitted with their original black marble fireplace mantels, are now filled with a suite of Duncan Phyfe Federal-period furniture with blue silk upholstery. Most of these pieces date from 1800 to 1820, earlier than the house, and probably are a bit overpowered by the huge scale of this Greek Revival suite of rooms. While I keep thinking that this furniture might look better in a smaller Federal-period house, I don't need any more houses (famous last words!). In any event, these Phyfe pieces still manage to look terrific, set off by the elegant window hangings, a Peale porthole portrait of George Washington over one mantel, a portrait of Andrew Jackson, by Ralph E. W. Earl, over the other mantel, plus other lesser-known portraits and prints. Atop the front parlor mantel is a rare French-made clock by *DuBuc á Paris* featuring a small statue of George Washington, inscribed "First in War, First in Peace, First in the Hearts of his Countrymen." There's an identical clock in the White House and also at Winterthur. Supposedly they were brought over from France by General Lafayette, in his triumphant return to America in 1824, as gifts to his friends. I found mine at Sotheby's many years ago.

Below, the George Washington Memorial Clock, by Dubuc á Paris, has a statue of Washington, an American Eagle, and the inscription: "Washington, First in War, First in Peace, First in the Hearts of his Countrymen." Early 19th century (c.1815).

A view of the double parlors
in the early 1980s showing
the original "royal blue" silk
fabric on furniture, since
replaced by a lighter color
blue. The window curtains
were designed by the late
David Richmond Byers of
Browne & Company in Atlanta,
shortly after he and Edward
Vason Jones had completed
the interior decoration of
The White House and
The State Department's new
Diplomatic Reception rooms.

Next two double page views:
The first floor Reception Room
probably served as an office for
Robert William Roper; Dining
Room, located in rear of first
floor for access to kitchen,
originally detached in rear

27

The ground floor of Roper House, also with high ceilings, is entered through a long hallway running the length of the house along the north side. There is a sweeping spiral staircase, ascending three floors, on the exterior side of this entrance hall. On the other side, two tall doors lead into a reception room in front and dining room on the rear, divided by double doors. The rooms can be thrown together en suite for large dinner parties. Both rooms are decorated in predominantly green and gold colors, with the green carpets seeming to flow right out to the lawn and garden just outside the floor-length windows. Behind the dining room as an outdoor patio overlooking the garden. This is my favorite place for breakfast or lunch when I am in Charleston.

The third, or top, floor is now returned to bedroom status, since I changed the living room in front from *pied-à-terre* days back into its original use as the master bedroom. From a big four-poster bed, one looks directly out to the Atlantic Ocean through tall windows that extend to the floor, with the original ornamental wrought-iron balconies framing the view. The sky blue curtains and carpet, which seem to merge with the blue-gray ocean outside, have given this bedroom the nickname "Blue Heaven." Also on the third floor, the second of two original bedroom suites has been turned into a library/television/reading room/lounge with comfortable, upholstered furniture (Duncan Phyfe not admitted here). On rainy, cold days in winter this room with a big fireplace, red draperies, and plenty of books is the place to be.

Once a bedroom, this third floor rear room has been turned into a library/television/reading room, with comfortable upholstered furniture. Portrait of Sir William Fraser is English, early 19th century (c.1820).

The third floor front room was undoubtedly the Ropers' master bedroom. The tall floor-to-ceiling windows provide a bird's-eye view out to Fort Sumter, where the Civil War began, and on to the Atlantic Ocean. The four-poster bed was used by Prince Charles on his four-day visit, and later by his sister, Princess Anne, on her later visit to Charleston.

General William Moultrie was a hero in the defense of Charleston in the American Revolution. Painted by Mather Brown, circa 1800.

Portrait of Mrs. Rawlins Lowndes, attributed to Thomas Sully. She was a Livingston from the Hudson Valley. One of four marriages between Lowndes of Charleston and Livingstons of New York.

The three floors of Roper House are connected by a red-carpeted spiral staircase. The goddesses of literature and music line the stairs.

The Rear Wing Addition — 1886

All the rooms that I have described are in the original 1838 block of Roper House, consisting of double parlors on each of the first two floors and a pair of large bedrooms on the third floor — all connected by the majestic circular staircase and hall. But there are many more rooms in a large rear wing, which was not added until 1886 following a disastrous earthquake that badly damaged most of Charleston. The "new wing," now over 125 years old, was built by the Rudolph Siegling family in a vote of confidence for Charleston's future after the earthquake. It is built on top of what was the original, detached kitchen of Roper House.

The new wing originally contained a kitchen and servants' quarters on the first floor, a sixty-foot-long, high-ceilinged ballroom on the second floor, and two more bedrooms on the third floor. Later, during the Depression of the 1930s, Roper House was sold by the Sieglings to Solomon Guggenheim, who converted the second floor ballroom wing into three more bedrooms. The wealthy Guggenheim, despite eliminating the handsome ballroom, was a good custodian of the house during the Depression years, when other Charleston houses deteriorated badly. Guggenheim, a mining magnate, was considered one of the nation's richest men at the time (he even built a huge iron vault on the first floor, evidently not fully trusting banks that were failing in the 1930s).

The three floors of the back porch of Roper House overlook the "new" rear wing, circa 1886 after the earthquake. The second floor provided a spacious ballroom during the 56-year occupancy of the Siegling family.

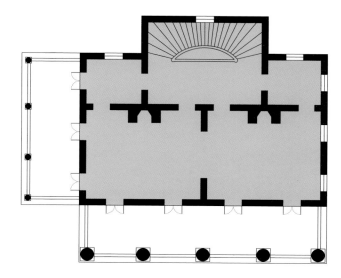

ROPER HOUSE
Floor Plan

The floor plan, used for all three floors of Roper House, highlights the popularity of symmetry, balance, and Palladian proportions during the American classical period of the early 19th century.

This garden view shows how the added rear wing attaches to the original (1838) block of Roper House. The ground floor porch provides a nice breakfast area overlooking the garden.

A garden view of Roper House in Spring. The unusual gazebo, used as a Tea House, was added during the 24-year residency of the Solomon Guggenheim family.

Ownership Changes Have Been Rare

In its now 175 years of existence, Roper House has had only a handful of owners, always a good sign that the house is a nice place to live. Robert William Roper, the builder, died in 1845 from malaria, and his widow, without children, sold the house in 1851 to the Ravenels, who lived next door. The house was uninhabitable during much of the Civil War because its harborside location was vulnerable to bombardment. The Rudolph Sieglings bought the house in 1874, right after the end of post-Civil War "Reconstruction" in South Carolina. They owned it for the next fifty-six years, adding the ballroom wing and repairing the earthquake's damage in 1886. The Guggenheims, who bought the house in 1929, kept up the house during the ravages of the Great Depression and World War II shortages. Drayton Hastie acquired the house in 1952. The Hasties maintained and loved the house during the post-World War II years before selling it to me in 1968. My forty-five years of ownership are exceeded in duration only by the Sieglings.

Unlike the situation at my other houses, remarkably few of the original Roper furnishings have found their way back home. In comparison with my experiences in restoring other houses, there are few traces of the Ropers at 9 East Battery, outside of the magnificent house itself. Mrs. Roper's portrait returned briefly after I rescued it from an attic and had the painting restored. But she was reclaimed several years later by a family member. I'm sure there's more Roper memorabilia out there somewhere!

Of all my houses, Roper House really looks and feels like a "party house" (hopefully not of the *Animal House* variety, although it looks suspiciously like a Greek fraternity house with those big columns). When I have given large parties here, the house works extremely well with crowds. Still the biggest party I have given here over the years was in connection with the grand opening of the rebuilt Mills House Hotel in downtown Charleston (I was the long-suffering lead investor). Over 400 guests, mostly Charlestonians and South Carolinians, but also many friends from North Carolina and New York, filled the lawn, all three floors and the roof. The house didn't even seem crowded. I noted that the most powerful politicians — Senators Thurmond

Another view of Roper House's spectacular three-story spiral staircase, lined with classical statuary.

and Hollings, four governors past and present, and the mayor — all found their way to the power point summit on the roof deck that moonlit evening. But what amazed me was how well traffic flowed within the house with such a large gathering. There were no bottlenecks; most rooms have more than one way of entering and exiting. The high ceilings on the principal floor swallow the noise and give a sense of grandeur, heightened by the house's original crystal chandeliers, which were originally gaslit. People seem to love to congregate on the big piazza opening off the double parlors on the second floor. At such times, the house seems alive and fulfilling its destiny.

The roof of Roper House was equipped with a deck by Mr. Jenrette in 1970, providing a nice view of Charleston's East Battery and the new Ravenel Bridge.

The *"best view in Charleston"*
from the roof-top deck of Roper
House. View looks eastward
past Fort Sumter located in the
mouth of Charleston's harbor.

A Magnet House for Charleston's Visitors

Roper House seems to be a stopping-off point for notables visiting Charleston. Mostly they come to see the house, not me! Distinguished visitors during my ownership include Presidents Ford and Bush, with their First Ladies, The Emperor and Empress of Japan, HRH The Prince of Wales, Lady Margaret Thatcher, General Colin Powell, Bishop Tutu from South Africa and assorted Rockefellers and Rothschilds. The house, with its tall Ionic columns invoking memories of Charleston's antebellum wealth, and the spectacular view out to sea never fails to impress.

Prince Charles' stay at Roper House, which lasted several days while he was in Charleston for a conference, was particularly memorable since he arrived only a few weeks after Hurricane Hugo, which had devastated Charleston (including my garden, which was literally swept away). Ernie Townsend, my extraordinary caretaker for more than 30 years, had wisely moved all the first floor furniture to the second floor before the storm hit. Chip Callaway, a landscape designer in Greensboro, North Carolina, then came to the garden's rescue, designing and installing a totally new garden (much improved) on short notice. The magnolia trees and palms he installed were so large they had to be delivered at 4:00 AM when there was no traffic. Under Ernie's supervision, the house had to be completely repainted and rewired on the first floor since five feet of seawater came into the house during the hurricane. But all's well that ends well. His Royal Highness and accompanying entourage seemed to enjoy their stay at 9 East Battery, which miraculously showed few signs of Hugo. The letter he wrote as a foreword to my book *Adventures with Old Houses* is included on page 53. Charles' sister, Princess Anne, also stayed at Roper House — at her brother's suggestion — while visiting Charleston a few years later.

Earnest Townsend, caretaker par excellence *of Roper House for Mr. Jenrette for more than 35 years. He was the hero of Hurricane Hugo, when five feet of sea water invaded the first floor of Roper House just weeks before Prince Charles' arrival.*

While visitors flock to Charleston in Spring, the City is even more glorious in Summer when crepe myrtle and oleander decorate the city in shades of red, pink, purple, and white colors — illustrated by this Summer view of Roper House.

HRH The Prince of Wales with Richard H. Jenrette at the Roper House in Charleston, South Carolina.

ST. JAMES'S PALACE

I first met Dick Jenrette in 1989 when he very generously offered me the use of his splendid Greek Revival mansion while I was in Charleston, South Carolina, for several days attending a conference for business people. What neither of us realised when I accepted his invitation was that Hurricane Hugo would make a devastating visit to Charleston a few weeks prior to my arrival. Mr. Jenrette's home overlooks Charleston harbour and the direct hit of the eye of the storm brought five feet of water into the first floor of the mansion and totally washed away the adjoining gardens.

Yet all was polished and serene by the time of my arrival.... Neither the necessity to repaint and rewire the entire first floor and replant the gardens, nor the time constraints could deter Mr. Jenrette from extending the gracious Southern hospitality for which Charleston is famed.

The Roper House, which takes its name from its builder in 1838, displays not only Mr. Jenrette's commitment to preserving the best of America's architectural heritage, but also his extraordinary collection of classical American art, antiques and other furnishings.

When I recognized several paintings in the house by the late Felix Kelly, whose work I admire and whose help I had sought in the past, of other early 19th Century houses in America, I learned that Roper House was only one of several great classical houses owned and restored by Mr. Jenrette. I understand that the total has now reached seven, not including others he has had a hand in restoring through various preservation groups in America. No wonder some of his admirers have described Dick as a one-person National Trust for Historic Preservation.

Since then I was pleased to learn that Dick has received the coveted Louise duPont Crowninshield Award, presented by the National Trust for his outstanding contribution to preserving America's architectural heritage. I was even more pleased to see that the Hadrian Award, which was presented to me by the World Monuments Fund several years ago, was awarded to Dick this past year.

Dick Jenrette's passion for classical architecture, and in sharing it with others, parallels my own interests in that and other forms of architecture in Britain and elsewhere. This book represents a fascinating personal memoir of how one person, while building several highly successful businesses, also found a fulfilling hobby in protecting and preserving his nation's architectural heritage. I hope the publication of this book will serve as an inspiration and guide to others to follow in his footsteps.

A House with Columns by the Sea

While Roper House seems to attract the rich and powerful when they come to Charleston and is wonderful for large parties, you don't have to have a lot of company — or *any* company — to enjoy this wonderful old mansion. What could be nicer than sipping the obligatory bourbon (when in Rome, do as Romans do!) on the piazza with its tall columns framing a view of the Atlantic ocean. Fragrant jasmine, pittosporum and lemon trees in the garden scent the breezes. The full moon never seems bigger to me than it does here, rising out of the Atlantic Ocean. The house is also magical on long summer evenings, when one feels the presence of the Old South.

There are so many memories here, not just in this house but in Charleston itself with its 350-year history — including hurricanes, an earthquake and two wars fought right here. The past may be too much with us in Charleston, but sometimes it's nice to get away from our high-tech world. Charleston is the perfect place to escape to a kinder, gentler life.

Rhett Butler had the same idea in the close of *Gone With the Wind* when Scarlett asked where he was going. He replied, "I'm going back to Charleston, back where I belong... I want to see if somewhere there isn't something left in life of charm and grace." I'd say he went to the right place!

This small desk provides a writing desk for Mr. Jenrette in his third floor bedroom. This book was mostly written here — with the view for inspiration.

PHOTO CREDITS

———

We are grateful to the following photographers for permission to use their photographs:

Rick Rhodes pages 8, 10, 13 (portrait of John Rutledge),
14-15, 16, 18, 20-21, 22, 24, 25, 28-29, 30-31, 34-35, 36, 37, 38, 40-41, 44, 46, 48-49, 54, back cover

Bruce Schwarz, pages 2, 6, 7, 42-43, 51

John M. Hall, pages 26-27, 32

Courtesy of Mr. Ash Milner, page 5 (vintage photograph)

Courtesy of the Charleston Area Convention and Visitors Bureau, page 50

Patrick Cox, page 13 (portrait of Martha Rutledge Roper). Collection of Martha Laurens Taylor

Courtesy of The Magazine *ANTIQUES, page 13 (portrait of Robert William Roper)*
Collection of John Laurens III and Patty Laurens Adams